MARTIN KERS
HOLLANDBOOK

Photographic Impressions of Holland

MARTIN KERS
HOLLANDBOOK

Photographic Impressions of Holland

Text: Marijke Kers

TRANSLATION: NEIL WALKER

SCHIPPER, PRINTERS-PUBLISHERS BV, LAREN (NH) / UITGEVERIJ TERRA ZUTPHEN BV

An introduction

Water, clouds and endless space, that's the Holland of Martin Kers. It is a beautiful country, and when you see his photographs, you realise how privileged you are to live here.
Many of his photographs feature low horizons and precisely symmetrical shapes. The mood of his works is determined by their colours. The natural colours of a country that has been built by its inhabitants. Take the dikes. Hand-built elevations separating the water from the land. Essential in the struggle to keep the one from invading the other. The dikes are a unique feature, particularly of the coastal and lowest lying areas. They form a razor sharp horizon right up close if you stand at the foot of one of them.
For centuries The Netherlands were, for the most part, waterlogged. But large tracts of water have since disappeared. We have drained the smaller inland lakes and ponds dry and reclaimed them to create places for us to live and work.
In the course of time, a lacelike network of rivers, canals, and thousands of duckweed and reed-filled ditches has evolved. In these same ditches minnows, frogs, roach, mint and flowering rushes abound. These are the ditches we know and love; we grew up with them.
Every region, every district, we created and built ourselves. We call it cultured country. Through Martin Kers' eyes we see it from way down low, close to the earth. From between the flowers and trees he looks at the distant and absolutely flat horizon which we've managed to retain even in the urban Randstad area.
Holland is not really tree country. And we're careful with the few ancient forests we still have. Particularly now that we have discovered how vulnerable trees are. Acid rain and over-fertilization have not passed us by. The large oak, beechwoods, the poplars planted in rows as windbreaks round isolated farms. The pine forests, the overgrown banks in the east, the pollard-willows in the west. Surely we're not going to lose all this?
All of us that live and work here help to shape our country, choose from alternatives, reclaim land and reconstruct our countryside. We construct roads, build new cities and determine the locations of schools, factories, and offices. More than any other nation we decide ourselves what the country we feel at home in is to look like.
The pride we have in the country we inherited from our forefathers is justified. When we, in turn, in ten or twenty years, hand over the baton to the next generation we must be able to say: "Take it from us, it's a fine country, keep it that way".
This enthralling book of photographs is about our country. Almost every day the famous photographer goes out to capture, in colour photographs, the moods of the Dutch landscape and everything that happens within it.
The dikes, fields, polders, pastures and especially the rivers, are for Martin Kers inexhaustable sources of inspiration. And the wonder of it all expresses itself in the mysterious colours and sharp perspectives of his photographs.
In every landscape there is only one vantage point from which to take the perfect picture, and Martin Kers, like no other, always knows how to find it. That is the secret of his unique series of photographs.

Dr. P. Winsemius

Photo: Ruth van Crevel

CULTURE

Holland is known throughout the world for its smooth, level landscape. Unlike almost every other European country, we have no mountains. Yet our country is less flat than we often realise.

The cruel ice age, a tropical sea, earthquakes and countless floods in the distant past have left visible traces across the landscape. These events created the low hills in the central, eastern and southern regions and, at one time, small lakes in the west. About ten thousand years ago the first settlers came to our still inhospitable land. They were shortly followed by the first of the farming communities and we are still today an agricultural society.

Since the beginnings of time some sixty million people have struggled with our unmanageable land and have, sometimes, changed it drastically. Marshes were drained, inland lakes were transformed into rich polder country and swampy peat moors have now become shimmering lakes.

The high and constantly changing waterlevel in and around the polders is controlled by a complicated system of dikes, canals, dams, locks and pumping stations.

There are few forests in The Netherlands. The majority of the surface is occupied by endless tracts of agricultural land, bulb fields and intensely green meadows, ditches straight as a die and serried lines of trees marching into the horizon. The paintings of the 17th century are famous for their impressive skies. Ruysdael and Hobbema were the masters of the game. The landscape changes constantly. Nothing stays the same except those magnificent skies. They are just as impressive now as when the old masters painted them. That's how they will remain, they are an indispensable part of the Dutch landscape.

THE BIESBOSCH POLDER / SOUTH HOLLAND

Farmers like to work efficiently and with purpose. Each corner or undulation is a bothersome obstacle. The plains drown the horizon, the land looks larger than life.

HILLEGOM / NORTH HOLLAND

For a brief but intense period in spring, the dry winter landscape changes into a colourful spectacle. Daffodils, hyacinths and many other flowers. But tulips remain the favorites.

NOORDBEEMSTER / NORTH HOLLAND

Not all bulb varieties flower at once. Sometimes they're cultivated to bloom row by row. Each bed has its own name and colour.

NOORDBEEMSTER / NORTH HOLLAND

It is the quality of the bulb in the ground that is vital. That's why the blooms have to be "picked" on time.

OUDENDIJK / NORTH HOLLAND

Land that was once the sea-bed is particularly suited to the cultivation of bulbs. Behind the perimeter dike the land is higher, dry and grassy with farms and cattle.

MIDDENBEEMSTER / NORTH HOLLAND

Cleverly and economically we divide the land by straight lines. Ditches, avenues of trees, roads, banks and bulb fields – march along side by side to the horizon. Only the shadows choose, at every hour of the day, to go their own way.

SINT MAARTEN / NORTH HOLLAND

Many of the new polders are used for bulb growing. The dike is an ideal grazing place for livestock.

KNARDIJK / FLEVOLAND

The Knardijk was the first supply road in the new polder. It became redundant when the polder was completed. Countless dandelions found here an undisturbed haven.

KIJK UIT / ZEELAND

It looks as though this land belongs to nobody. No grazing cow, no farmer to thrust his spade into the ground. Then wonders occur. Poppies and camomile take over, hundreds of thousands of them.

FLEVOLAND

At the edge of the wood was a meadow, as green as grass. But in May it turned yellow and that was something very special.

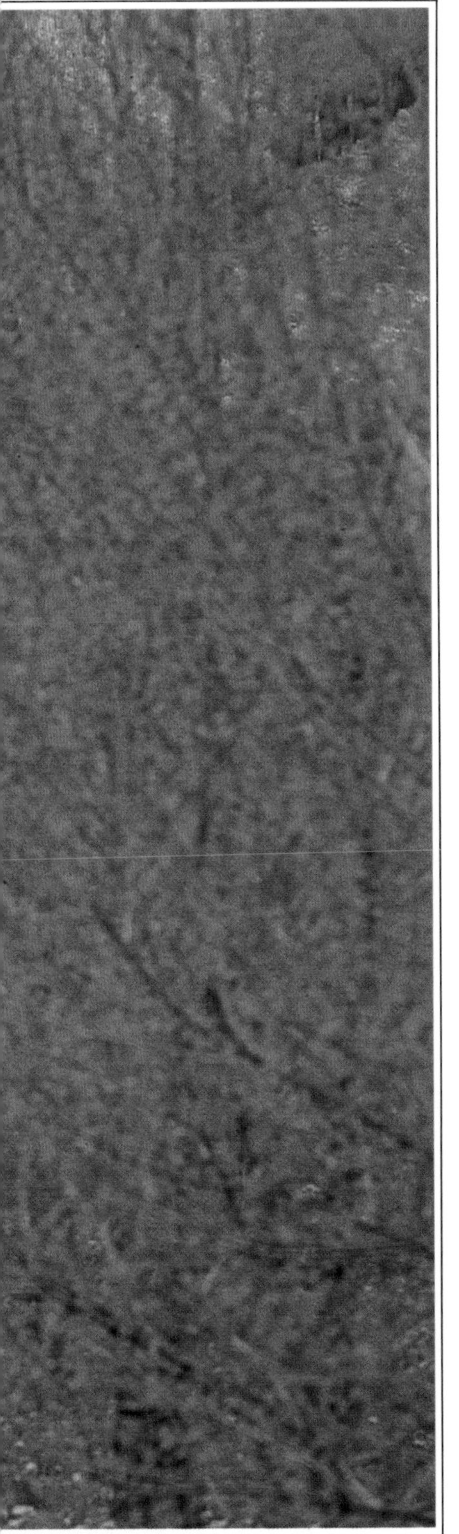

HOBREDE / NORTH HOLLAND

Clouds come and go, they create themselves. The land is manmade. Just the way man wants it.

WESTHOEK / FRIESLAND

The arable land appears to be limitless. Yet it ends somewhere. The encompassing ditch makes a turn and the land follows it willingly.

OOSTERBIERUM / FRIESLAND

Each ditch has been dug. Each piece of land measured. The seed has been sown. But the reeds come of their own free will, wished for or not.

LITTENSERADEEL / FRIESLAND

First light is barely breaking. Figures and houses are creeping into view. The horizon will soon be visible. The land grows and reveals its secrets.

CASTRICUM / NORTH HOLLAND

Dusk is falling apace. Soon the last train will pass. Then the night, still and peaceful till the first morning light appears again.

EILANDSPOLDER / NORTH HOLLAND

Formerly an island between the Schermer and the Beemster. Taken over by godswit, snipe and redshank. And when the day's as young as this the cows just stand there steaming.

DRIEHUIZEN / NORTH HOLLAND

Trees, roads, plots and ditches, they all begin on the drawing board. Country planning they call it. Later the dragline and the asphalt machine follow the lines of the plan to the centimeter.

KOEDIJK / NORTH HOLLAND

No flower, no seedpod, not even a bird decorates the winter landscape. But the heavens are painted the brightest of hues.

SINT MAARTEN / NORTH HOLLAND

A tight bend is where the dike is at its strongest. This section will withstand any flood. And the land follows its every whim and every curve.

CORNWERD / FRIESLAND

Immediately behind the high dike along the IJsselmeer the landscape unfolds like an immeasurable carpet. The wind grabs its chance. Those that live here do so behind the cover of close-packed trees.

TEXEL

Sparrows have almost human characteristics. Lively, squabbling and talkative.

SCHELLINKHOUT / NORTH HOLLAND

High up on the dike, with your back to what used to be the sea, you look out over the soggy land. Black-headed gulls, dabchicks, grebes and water-rail live here. If you're lucky you can hear the large reedwarbler cry out "karkiet, karkiet".

WIJHE / OVERIJSSEL

The river meanders its way across the land. In the summer a lovely stream with green banks. But in the autumn transformed to a broad, angry torrent that obliterates the meadows.

DEIL / SOUTH HOLLAND

The pale "Anquitaine", an exceptionally good-looking breed of cow from France, grazes peacefully not far from the busy Deil intersection. Chefs from the Exquise restaurant say these Anquitaines provide the tastiest steaks.

DRIEHUIZEN / NORTH HOLLAND

The wayward flood-tide used to follow the movements of this land in formation. The sea has long since vanished but the curves of erosion remain.

DRONTEN / FLEVOLAND

Our newest territories, only a few decades old. The ugly newness softens. Saplings become trees behind which the horizon shelters. Thus infinity gains a human dimension.

ECHTEN / FRIESLAND

Nothing changes like a hayfield. High grass, many trees. After the harvest everything becomes golden yellow. Below, the stubble withers into a hundred shades of green.

ZEEUWS-VLAANDEREN / ZEELAND

Lumpy, rough and earthy. It is late September, the beet campaign has begun.

BAARD / FRIESLAND

The Friesians don't like trees. They are unprofitable obstructions. It looks like a prairie but tidy, tasteful and organized.

WIERINGERMEER / NORTH HOLLAND

The roads are like the avenues of trees and ditches, straight as a die. Even the houses stand tidily side by side in line.

SCHARNEGOUTUM / FRIESLAND

A plain is never plainer than when the wind blasts it unhindered at nightfall.

DEN BURG / TEXEL

This special breed is called the "Texel". Many relatives of these have been shipped to South Africa, South America and Mexico.

POLDER RONDE HOEP / NORTH HOLLAND

The Waver, the Amstel and the Drecht canal encircle a polder just south of Amsterdam. Its only inhabitants, some livestock and a few birds.

VERDRONKEN LAND VAN SAEFTINGE / ZEELAND

Just inside the ring dike – an unusual meeting at an unusual point.

MANTGUM / FRIESLAND

Twice a week military jets invade the peace. For the cows it's merely milking time. Same day, same time, same place.

LOPIKERKAPEL / UTRECHT

Winter grazing along the Lek. The rising mists bathe the landscape in an eerie light.

HARLINGEN / FRIESLAND

A lucky moment along a narrow country lane near Kimswerd. Deer. But hold your breath, before you can say "Jack Robinson" they vanish from view.

WATER

In The Netherlands water comes in all shapes and sizes. Large rivers and minute streams, lakes, fens, canals, ditches and rivulets.

They all came about in different ways and serve very different needs. Take canals, they have always been excavated. Almost all the lakes are a result of peat-digging. And every field and meadow has its ditch. Any town of consequence has its position by a river to thank for its fame. Water used to provide the fastest mode of transport. Import and export of goods was quicker and safer by boat. Woudrichem, Dordrecht, Kampen and Amsterdam grew prosperous on water traffic. But water is also our enemy. Storms and spring tides drive the seawater up the rivers and deep into the countryside, with predictable results.

Know thy enemy, it is said. On the Dam Square in Amsterdam there is a sign, a watermark that indicates sea level to within a few centimeters.

This is the norm against which all other ground- and water levels are measured. The degree to which local land or water levels differ from it determines what action needs to be taken by locks, dikes, pumps and dams.

SINT MAARTEN / NORTH HOLLAND

Severe floods leave their mark on the landscape. Long after the flood has subsided and the breach in the dike has grown over, small, deep lakes remain.

SOUTH BEVELAND / ZEELAND

Small, deep, lakes nestling up to a dike are called "wielen" or "welen". They are the result of earlier breaches.

GROTE PEEL / NORTH BRABANT

Peat bogs and fens, the last truly wild part of the country. Prehistoric landscape cared for as a nature reserve.

TJEUKEMEER / FRIESLAND

The Tjeukemeer is one of the eight great lakes of southwest Friesland. All a result of peat digging.

BIESBOSCH / NORTH BRABANT

Extensive area of reeds, water and river shrubs. Important winter retreat and breeding reserve for marine and migrating birds.

HARINGVLIET / SOUTH HOLLAND

The Haringvliet was formerly a danger area with its rising and falling tides. The Haringvliet Dam, part of the Deltaplan, brought this to an end.

DRIMMELEN / NORTH BRABANT

You can reach the Biesbosch via the river Amer. This exceptional area of natural beauty was created by the Elisabeth floods of 1421.

OOSTVAARDERSPLASSEN / FLEVOLAND

Reluctant land that after the polder was dug refused to accept its new role. Now this unique nature reserve has been taken over by thousands of birds.

PINGJUM / FRIESLAND

Friesland is known for its large lakes. Less well-known are the innumerable watercourses and canals that search an anonymous path through the flat countryside.

IJSSELMEER / FRIESLAND

Enkhuizen as a mirage seen from Friesland. In certain weather conditions, the entire town floats free of the horizon.

DREUMEL / GELDERLAND

The Waal overflows its banks. Uiterwaarden, now wet, now dry. Only the willows can withstand such extremes.

DREUMEL / GELDERLAND

Within the dikes each drop of water is controlled. Outside nature can run riot. Then wonders never cease.

WAAL / GELDERLAND

In a land of large rivers the Waal is one of the most important. Sometimes broad, sometimes calm and sometimes turbulent.

OPENLUCHTMUSEUM / ARNHEM

Land and water can also become history. Then they meet in a museùm.

IJSSEL / GELDERLAND

Sailing on the IJssel is a joy. Floating for a hundred kilometers, past winding banks with narrow dikes.

EERNEWOUDE / FRIESLAND

Formerly peat country, here deep, there soggy-shallow.
Skûtsjes and the Frisian waters are inseparably linked.

ALEM / GELDERLAND

A clumsy twist in the Maas. The freighters have not been here for years. It's now a peaceful spot to fish.

HOBREDE / NORTH HOLLAND

Drainage canals in the Zeevang polder. They rarely have a name.

SNEEKERMEER / FRIESLAND

Skûtsjes are wooden freight and shuttle boats of the nineteenth century. Each year they race each other for ten days and end up with a party.

WADDENZEE

On a fine day and in sight of the harbour the sea appears friendly and peaceful.

NORTH SEA

The sea seems endless. The ferry knows the way and takes you effortlessly to foreign shores.

AFSLUITDIJK / IJSSELMEER

Where there is water, there is a shore. Often decorated with bollards, breakers and piers.

BIESBOSCH / NORTH BRABANT

Bushes, reeds and willows with lots of water in the former freshwater delta. A unique area of great natural beauty you can only approach by boat.

GIETHOORN / OVERIJSSEL

Exhaustive peat-digging in previous centuries resulted in a complicated network of minute canals navigable only by special narrow punts.

VERENIGD KANAAL / GRONINGEN

Canals are not a natural phenomenon. They are always dug by hand or machine.

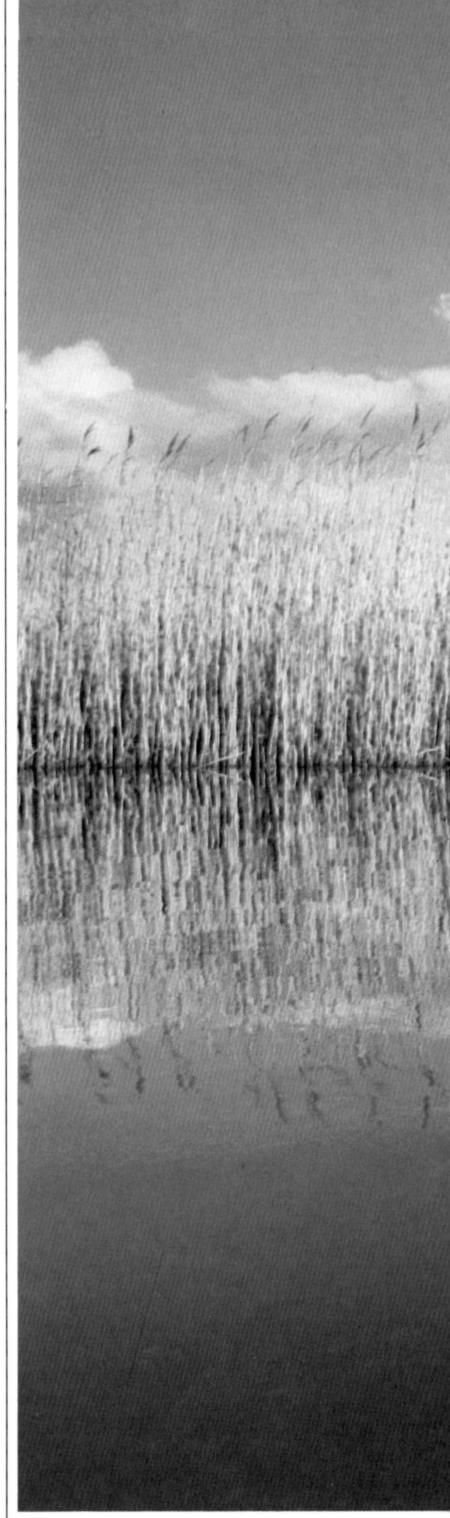

SINT MAARTEN / NORTH HOLLAND

A breached dike causes deep pockets in the land. Pits full of water that struggle slowly to become land again.

FLEVOLAND

In our newest polders all the waterways are handmade.

PIAAM / FRIESLAND

The level of the water in the polder is controlled by pumping engines in the IJsselmeerdijk from where it is carried further by nameless watercourses.

HOLLE POARTE / IJSSELMEER

Each year several hundred swans set down along the IJsselmeerdijk and the Afsluitdijk.

SCHERMERHORN / NORTH HOLLAND

Redevelopment of the land. And for a while puddles of mud and rainwater appear.

TJEUKEMEER / FRIESLAND

Most Frisian lakes are the result of peat-digging. The dried peat was then used in the big cities as fuel.

LINGE / GELDERLAND

A modest stream that rises near Kasteel Doornenburg. It meanders along in search of the Waal.

MAAS / NORTH BRABANT

The Maas is the most southerly river of the central Dutch river area. And the natural boundary between Utrecht and North Brabant.

CORNWERD / IJSSELMEER

The coming of the Afsluitdijk signaled the end of the Zuiderzee. Ebb and flood were stilled. And the former sea developed all the characteristics of a lake.

APELDOORNS KANAAL / GELDERLAND

Members of the Ardeidea (heron) family inhabit the entire world with the exception of the North and South poles.

MAKKUM / FRIESLAND

So close to the water is Makkum that its character is determined by boats – of all types and in all sizes.

OUDENDIJK / NORTH HOLLAND

Canals come in all sizes. One thing they all have in common is their uncompromising straightness, their total lack of corners.

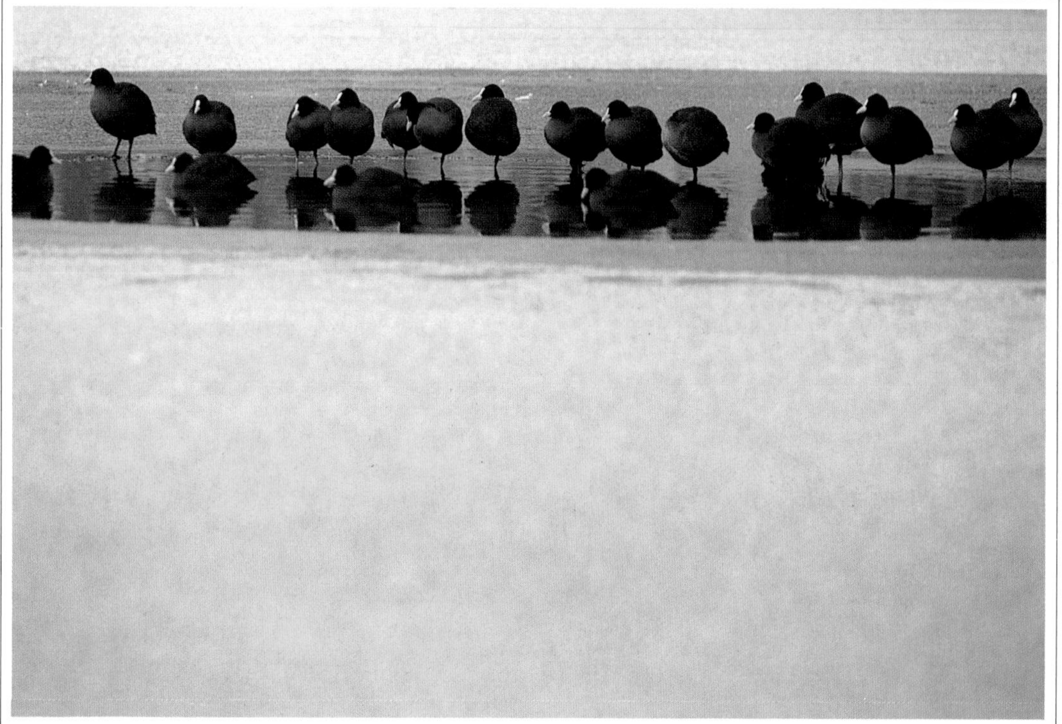

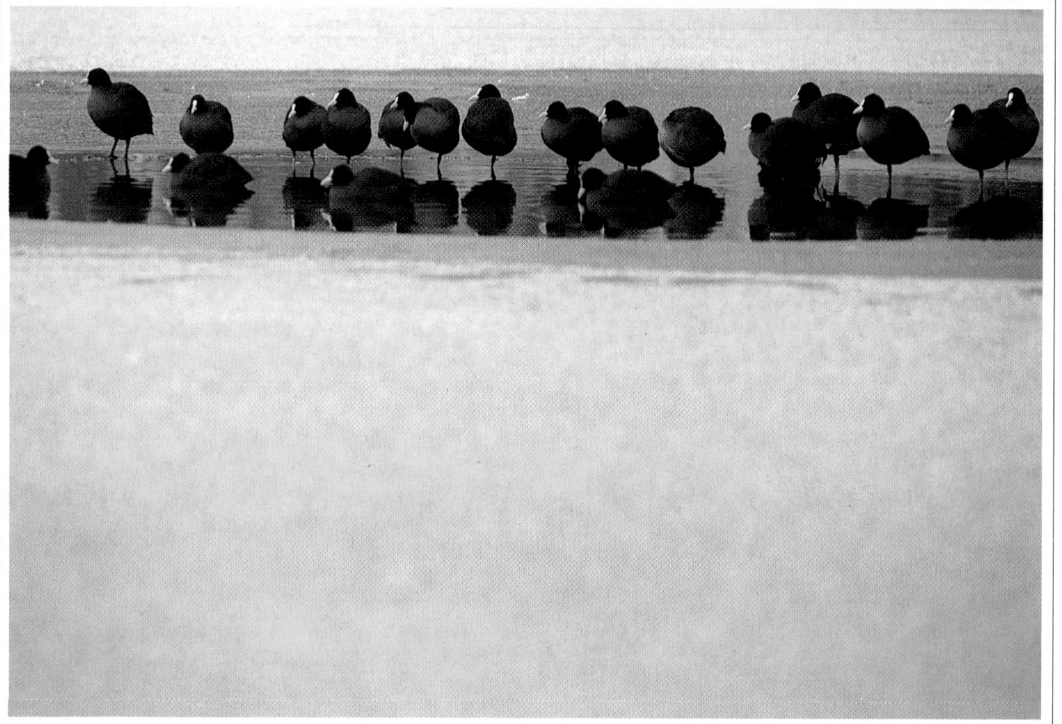

IJSSEL / GELDERLAND

The banks of the IJssel are bird-filled again. Many breeds migrate to warmer climates. Except busy little black-headed gulls, they're always around.

VLIST / SOUTH HOLLAND

Especially in the winter the coots huddle together. Then make their way in great flocks over the land and over the ice in search of food.

BALINGER EN MANTINGERZAND / DRENTHE

Fens in a nature reserve of sand and heather. For years geologists have been puzzling over how these minute lakes were created.

COASTLINE

The Netherlands is a low-lying country that nestles behind hundreds of kilometers of long pale dikes. Behind the dikes an unpredictable North Sea roars. Usually the waves roll gently onto our white beaches. In a storm the raging surf lashes vulnerable dunes that resist the attack with difficulty.
Vast quantities of sand are picked up and blown to unknown destinations.
The beaches and dunes march along the coast to the Wadden islands. There especially the dunes become untamed nature reserves, constantly subject to the shifting influences of wind and water.
The two most northerly provinces have almost no sand along their coastlines. A solid dike, Delta high, protects the land there. Over the dike the ground is soft and smooth and fruitful. The ebb tide leaves behind great tracts of dry mud-flat. This means it's time for the thousands of birds to feed. They are dependent for their livelihood on this rare piece of nature reserve.
On May 28th 1932, the last gap in the Afsluitdijk was filled in. At that moment the raging North Sea became a peaceful inland sea. Ebb and flood ceased, causing great changes in nature's pattern. The Netherlands lost great lengths of coastline. A shame really since the rising and falling tides give rise twice daily to the opportunity for discovering fascinating sights. The land alternates from dry to drenched. Flocks of birds, strange insects and very special plants can be found. A tidal region is constantly changing, never giving boredom a chance.

TERSCHELLING

Coast in the evening. The wind has died down. Almost unnoticed the border between land and sea shifts back and forth.

JULIANADORP / NORTH HOLLAND

A beach is not just a beach after the storm.

TERSCHELLING

An unbridled meeting of sand, sea and wind. They take it in turns to win the battle.

MAASVLAKTE / SOUTH HOLLAND

Millions of cubic meters of pumped land. Europoort, Europe's port, a professionally created frontier port. Who will live there, work there, play there?

SCHOORL / NORTH HOLLAND

Posts, 40 of them, waiting for the summer and for the pavillions that they'll support the summer season long.

WADDENKUST / FRIESLAND

The Waddenzee is an inland sea without breakers. The water level rises and falls gently at the foot of the dike.

HARLINGEN / FRIESLAND

A heavenly show above the sea. It's brief, so don't be late... or early.

WESTHOEK / FRIESLAND

The water has left for good. Land homesick for the sea.

HOLWERD / FRIESLAND

Sodden, shallow, lonely, deserted. What is a mud-flat?

WADDENKUST / FRIESLAND

Pioneering marsh samphire in the country's nature reserve along the coast of Friesland and Groningen provinces. Important to ornithologists internationally.

IJSSELMEER / RODE KLIF

In the winter the water freezes to a mirror-smooth ice plain. Then you can skate to the horizon and beyond.

MAASVLAKTE / SOUTH HOLLAND

Artificial off-shore sandspit. Inhospitable but a hive of activity. The whole world bustles back and forth.

TEXEL

Sand, sea and wind. The elements at play. He who wishes to, joins in.

WESTHOEK / FRIESLAND

The sea appears tamed, the waves are silent far from the coast.

IJSSELMEER

Clear water becomes clear ice as it drops below freezing point.

TERSCHELLING

Those from Terschelling call this the off-season. No people, dogs, rabbits... or birds.

KOEHOOL / FRIESLAND

Salt-marsh, mud-flat. The flood-tide deposits mud. The ebb carries it back to the sea. Is the land turning into water or the water into land?

DOLLARD / GRONINGEN

Striding happily through a squelchy layer of mud supported by an unseen firm layer below.

TERSCHELLING

Shell bank, essential element in the food supply chain.

SCHIERMONNIKOOG

.Sometimes a ship sails off-course. If it succumbs to the elements then it's time for the inevitable and efficient salvage work.

TERSCHELLING

Every piece of flotsam tells a story. Has someone been washing the Waddenzee?

TERSCHELLING

Sometimes you find strange things on the beach, things you've never seen before. Unknown shapes and forms, secret and forbidding.

IJSSELMEER / AFSLUITDIJK

There is always fish. Every day the nets are set out to catch them. Every day the fishermen sails by to empty them.

WIJK AAN ZEE / NORTH HOLLAND

Resorts along the coast. Bustle and amusement last the whole summer season.

TEXEL

Refreshment at the foot of the dike.

TEXEL

All the Dutch coastal dunes are managed as nature reserves. Walkers have to abide by strict rules.

DUNE RESERVE / NORTH HOLLAND

White poplars along the coast. Their ability to thrive in the salty sea air is legendary.

MEIJENDEL / SOUTH HOLLAND

Bent-grass is essential for the maintenance of the dunes. The roots creep invisibly beneath the sand to depths of five meters, thus preventing it from being blown away.

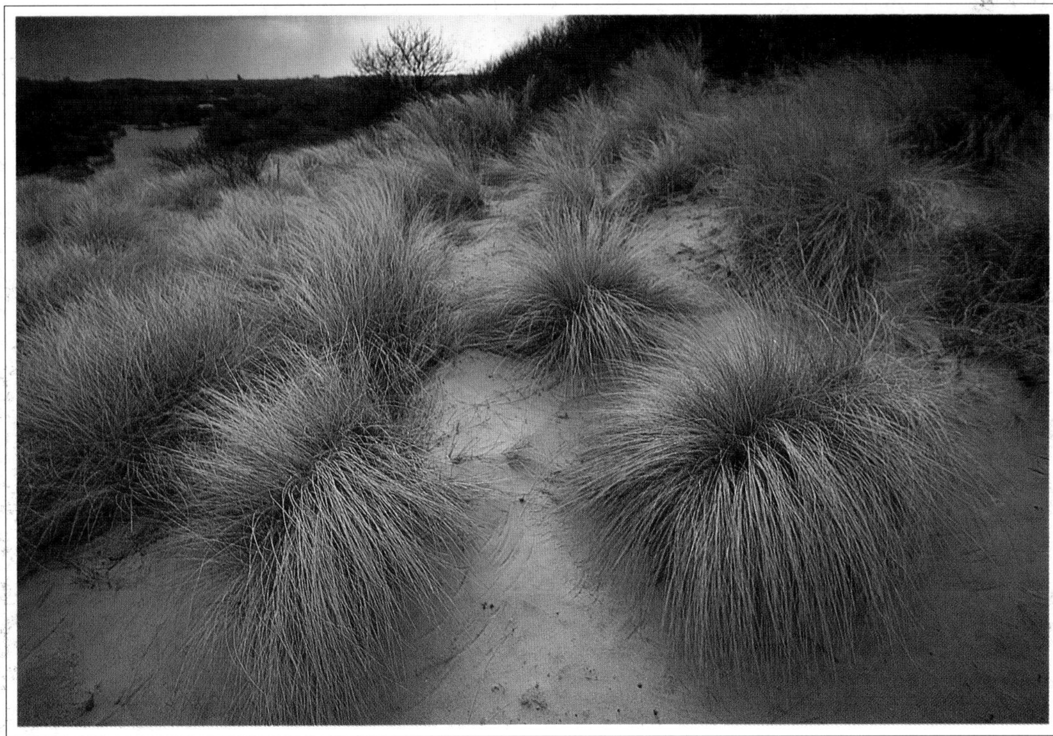

DIKES

Rivers, lakes and seas have a tendency to overrun their banks. The water floods the land, casting terror into the hearts of those who live there. Innumerable times our land has been invaded by storm and tempest. Villages were swept away. People and cattle were drowned.

Some 1000 years ago monks found a solution to the problem of too much water. They invented the dike, long caterpillar-like walls of sand, clay and stones as the barrier between land and water. Dikes that could withstand the encroaching water, keeping the land dry.

An ingenious invention that we are using to this day. Nowhere in The Netherlands is there a spot where the waters have a chance to invade the land at an embarrassing moment.

The dikes are mostly broad, high and strong. Yet they have been known to breach. The last time it happened was in 1953. A disaster. Many people and livestock perished. ''Never again'', we said, and developed the Delta plan. Almost everywhere in The Netherlands the dikes were raised. And in Zeeland, our most vulnerable province, a complicated system of dams, locks and flood tide defenses was built that the whole world comes to wonder at. Now many dikes have become redundant. They proved their worth holding back the sea in the past. The waters have now been professionally diverted and nobody has the energy to tear down such dikes.

Happily, since they provide wonderful views over the countryside to those who walk or ride their tops.

OOSTERDIJK / NORTH HOLLAND

Lighthouses stand along the coast of the IJsselmeer at regular distances from each other. Beacons in the night for shipping.

DRIEHUIZEN / NORTH HOLLAND

To walk along the dike is to follow the old floodline of a former inland sea. Now the polder is called Schermer.

WORKUM / FRIESLAND

Inaccessible, yet reassuring, the IJsselmeerdijk in the background.

HARLINGEN / FRIESLAND

Countless steps high above land and water. A beautiful footpath without end.

MEGEN / NORTH BRABANT

Dams and locks elsewhere in the Maas guarantee the safe control of water, but dikes are far from redundant. You never know.

's-GRAVENDEEL / SOUTH HOLLAND

Trees rarely grow on a functioning dike. The growing, searching, roots can cause much damage. Birds are another story.

WADDENDIJK / FRIESLAND

The sea dikes are cherished and carefully nurtured for attacks from the sea are violent and pitiless.

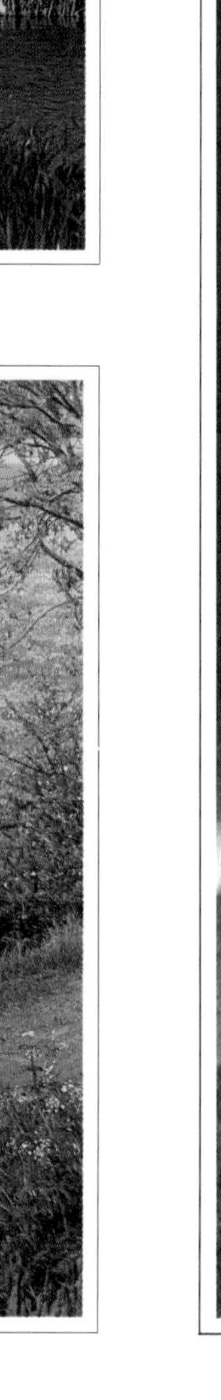

SCHERMERHORN / NORTH HOLLAND

The water level of the Beemsteringvaart is higher than the neighbouring land. Some careful water management is called for.

NEERIJNEN / GELDERLAND

Behind the dike the river has long since been tamed. It has lost the strength to flood the land. Nestling up to such a dike makes one feel safe and protected.

KOEHOOL / FRIESLAND

A thousand years of experience. By now we know how.
Building dikes like impregnable fortresses.

RILLAND / ZEELAND

Rows of trees atop a tall dike act as windbreaks for vulnerable fruit trees. But they remind one of the lapping of the waves in the distant past.

NEDERHEMERT SOUTH / GELDERLAND

Dikes that no longer offer resistence to the tides offer succour to trees.

OUDEBILDTDIJK / FRIESLAND

Reclaiming land from the sea. On the edge of Friesland you can still see how it's done. Every few centuries a new dike a couple of kilometers into the sea. The older dike has been converted into a residential area.

LEK / UTRECHT

The volume of melted ice and rainwater determine the water level in the Lek.

JAARSVELD / UTRECHT

Important inland waterway to and from Rotterdam. Evening falls putting a stop to traffic for the day.

PETTEN / NORTH HOLLAND

What used to be sea is now called Hazepolder. Sheep now graze where once eels were caught.

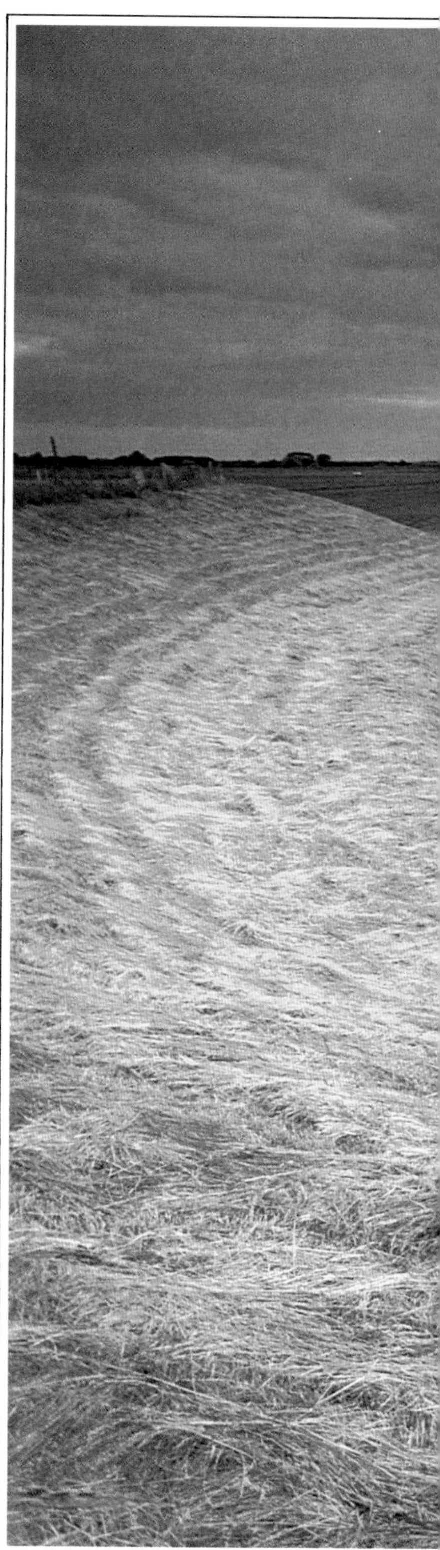

WESTFRIESE OMRINGDIJK / NORTH HOLLAND

The massive dikes remind one of the massive efforts that went into their construction.

BOTSHOL / UTRECHT

Between the dikes is the Amstel and polder, and the sparkling waters of the Vinkeveenseplassen. An ideal summer resort.

WESTFRIESE OMRINGDIJK /
NORTH HOLLAND

The longest and oldest dike in The Netherlands is still very nearly intact. A historical monument almost 1000 years old.

DEN HELDER / NORTH HOLLAND

Some dikes have south-facing slopes, just like mountains. Ideal nestling places for certain families of flowers.

SCHAGEN / NORTH HOLLAND

Dikes have windward and leeward sides. On the windward side, flowers bloom whose fluffy seeds were blown there.

SINT MAARTEN / NORTH HOLLAND

Taraxum officinalis – Better known as dandelion. In a week's time the dike will be white with their tufted clocks.

ZUID BEVELAND / ZEELAND

Many of the one thousand-year-old dikes have been converted to nature reserves in microcosm. They encircle minute fields and meadows.

WAALDIJK / GELDERLAND

Whenever old dikes are left alone, flowers take over the former sea defences.

BLOEMDIJKEN / ZEELAND

A network of narrow mini-dikes. In the spring, infested by clouds of cow parsley. The dikes belong to a variety of preservation organisations.

WAARDENBURG / GELDERLAND

Weak early morning light rises above the waterscape on the edge of Tielerwaard.

LINGE / GELDERLAND

Depending on the lie of the land very substantial differences in vegetation can occur, even quite close to each other.

HOOGEBEINTUM / FRIESLAND

Mounds, like dikes, were there to hold back the tides. All the way to Denmark you can find such lowly hills.

KOEHOOL / FRIESLAND

The biggest dikes are the sea dikes. The tops of such dikes must be high enough to prevent the spray of storm waves from encroaching on the land.

LAUWERSOOG / GRONINGEN

Beneath the dike, along the water line. Bicycle paths like this are rare in The Netherlands.

KORNWERDERZAND / FRIESLAND

The Waddenzee lies behind the dike. The view from the top intrigues at every season of the year.

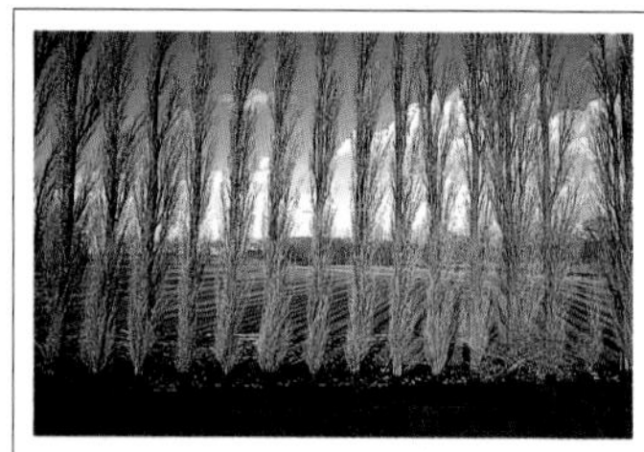

TREES

Beeches, birches, oaks, alders, willows and poplars are natural inhabitants of our country. They can withstand the dampness of our climate.
All types of trees have their own characteristics and these, over time, we have recognized and learnt to use. Poplars to help the land retain its moisture and for making logs. Alder and willow branches were, in the distant past, the only means of keeping the baker's fires burning.
In all Europe only Ireland has fewer trees than The Netherlands. There is, of course, a reason for this. Our country has so often been flooded by sea water and there are not many trees capable of withstanding such treatment. In addition, much of The Netherlands consisted largely of water and sparsely wooded country. Polders have always been used for agricultural and cattle breeding purposes, never planted with trees. The central and eastern areas of The Netherlands are less low-lying. Floods have no chance here. And here's where trees abound.

The Veluwe is our largest area of woodland. It is managed by a number of preservation agencies. It was particularly in the East that wealthy, priviledged, individuals in previous centuries, established large estates. Most of these have been purchased by the Forestry Commission, National Trust and Regional Preservation societies. They manage and maintain these national treasures, these densely wooded parklands, and guarantee us all the chance to enjoy them.

EDESE BOS / GELDERLAND

Beechwoods are rare in The Netherlands. Yet beech is an indigenous species and every stretch of deciduous wood has its beech.

FLEVOLAND

No plan for the future of the land is complete without woods. Though trees have a hard time taking root in sea clay.

FLEVOLAND

Spring came and saw and conquered somewhere along a deserted cart-track.

SLENAKEN / LIMBURG

The pollard-willow is popular all over The Netherlands. No ditch is complete without pollard-willow along its banks.

ZUID BEVELAND / ZEELAND

In neat and tidy rows, the poplars, elms or willows follow every curve of the dike.

NOORBEEK / LIMBURG

Poplars grow quickly and provide us with useful timber. The main reason for such widespread planting of this type has been economic.

ZUID BEVELAND / ZEELAND

Redundant dikes, richly endowed with trees and rare plants.

WELSUM / OVERIJSSEL

Limes can become hundreds of years old. Give a lime the chance and it will grow into an impressive monument.

SINT GEERTRUID / LIMBURG

At significant points in the landscape oaks or horse chestnuts are planted as if to point the way. Later the trees take on a religious significance.

HOOGCRUTS / LIMBURG

Trees too are doomed to die. Some are felled, others fall foul of disease or are toppled by the winds.

One seldom finds beechwoods in The Netherlands. Nearby Biddinghuizen one is growing, young, pure and vulnerable.

LEUVENUM / GELDERLAND

Green, grey, and brown are the colours of woodland. The light of a late autumn day has its own way with colour.

WINTERSWIJK / GELDERLAND

The east of the country has the most trees. Ancient lanes of trees remind us of the estates of blue-blooded families.

WINTERSWIJK / GELDERLAND

Such splendidly decorative landscapes are to be found in the oldest inhabited areas.

ELSPEET / GELDERLAND

Trees provide wood – for all sorts of purposes. Even for burning in the grate.

ACHTERHOEK / GELDERLAND

The pattern of root growth often mirrors that of the branches. The beech's roots are smooth and slender, just like its branches.

NIERSEN / GELDERLAND

Beeches are stately and impressive. Perfect landmarks for the graceful drive leading to an imposing estate.

HOGE VELUWE / GELDERLAND

The Hoge Veluwe is one large, interconnecting woodland. Almost all varieties of tree are to be found there.

OPENLUCHTMUSEUM / GELDERLAND

Beeches have small, firm, leaves. All the same colour. Yet in the autumn, each leaf takes on its own particular hue.

KLAASWAAL / SOUTH HOLLAND

Thanks to the frequent floods there are practically no woods in the southwest provinces. Tall rows of trees have been planted to protect the crop of the endless polders.

METSLAWIER / FRIESLAND

Elms are tough trees. They can withstand the rigours of the elements better than most. That's why the elm is Friesland's favourite.

MIDDENBEEMSTER / NORTH HOLLAND

Once polder land is created an exterior dike becomes an inland dike. Then it is planted with trees and becomes a wind-break.

OOSTERWIERUM / FRIESLAND

In sparcely populated areas the church became a haven in times of need. High elms protected this place, particularly the tower, from wind and weather.

KAMERIK / UTRECHT

Pollard-willows need a lot of attention. Every twelve years every branch must go, to avoid the crown becoming too heavy and the tree toppling.

TRITZUM / FRIESLAND

Such a wall of leafless trees seems gentle and highly vulnerable. In fact it is tough, indestructable and protective.

LOPIKERKAPEL / UTRECHT

In the river delta the soil is damp and swampy. Poplars grow here happily. Just occasionally elms take root and can show the world what they are capable of.

ZOUTKAMP / GRONINGEN

The people from Groningen are not real tree fanciers. But if they do plant one you can bet it will be an elm.

QUATRE BRAS / GELDERLAND

Poplars in which to invest. Appreciable return in less than twenty years.

KOOTWIJKERZAND / GELDERLAND

Big pines feel at home in rough, wild, country. Their winged seeds travel far. Hence their name, winged pines.

KOOTWIJKERZAND / GELDERLAND

In areas of loose sand one has to be careful that the ground isn't blown from underfoot.

GROLLOO / DRENTHE

Fir plantations are efficient and profitable. They are a common sight in the poorer soils of Drenthe, where they are planted as an investment.

ENVIRONMENT

Here stands a house. Further up, another. Between them a road. There's a field too, a meadow with cows and sheep. And roads leading to them.
Again more houses, meadows and fields. Roads crossing each other. Road signs, lane-change signs, traffic lights, rules and police.
Roads cross rivers. Tunnels, viaducts, swing bridges and draw-bridges. We make this and we make that. And call it production. Factories, stockpiling, cars and barges, power stations, telephone, harbours and offices.
We play games and sports, preferably on the water. From start to finish, sailing, swimming and skating. Tribunes and large crowds. More people, better quality, speed is the essence.
Dig canals, right through the countryside. Rows of trees and rows of houses side by side in endless lines. Trains, stopping trains, express trains, engines and intercities. Gleaming rails, level crossings, sections, stations, signals, barriers.

LOPIKERWAARD / UTRECHT

Low-lying polder behind the high Lek dike. Tidily and carefully measured even to the smallest garden.

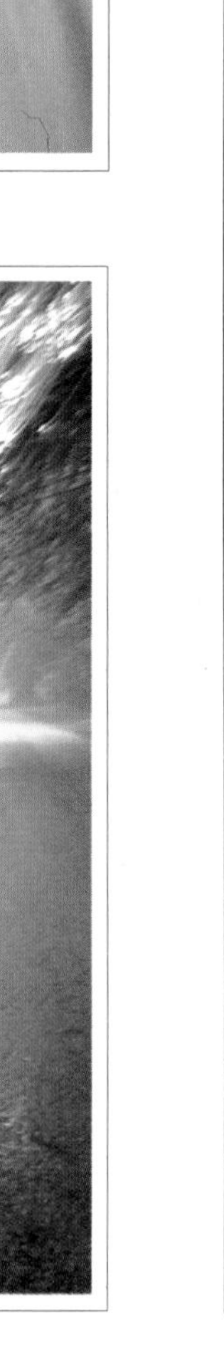

TERMUNTERZIJL / GRONINGEN

A lock keeps apart the waters of the Eemswater and the lower-lying Termunterzijldiep. There you can sail, and play.

GORTEL / GELDERLAND

Woods are reservoirs of oxygen and game, and biotopes for birds, boar and beetles. But also walking country for people.

FRANEKER / FRIESLAND

The edge of the town creeps outwards. Peaceful meadows make way for protected residential areas. All except that one small field that got left behind.

LYNDEN / NORTH HOLLAND

Along the banks of the canal the houses and trees march in line towards a pretty village. The water stamps its mark on the shape of this little community.

PEKELA / GRONINGEN

Many moons ago the Pekelerhoofddiep was dug for its peat. Today the barge traffic is grateful for its existence.

WEESP / NORTH HOLLAND

Right up close to Amsterdam South-East can be found the rural peace of the banks of the Gein.

DELFZIJL / GRONINGEN

Delfzijl is the sixth busiest harbour in the country. Straw and board are shipped out and coal makes its way back.

BROUWERSDAM / SOUTH HOLLAND

The building of the Brouwersdam shut the Grevelingen off from the North Sea for good. At the water's edge stands Rinus. A comforting thought.

ADUARDERZIJL / GRONINGEN

North Netherlands, few wish to live here. Minute villages, here and there a farm and agricultural land stretching past the horizon.

132

ZUIDERMEER / NORTH HOLLAND

Many times a day the Hoorn-Alkmaar train rushes past the tiny village. It never stops there, there's no station.

BATH / ZEELAND

The Schelde-Rhine Canal links the harbour of Antwerp with the Dutch waterway network. The high bridge connects Bath with the peaceful country beyond.

PINGJUM / FRIESLAND

Farmer's hut or second home? A panoramic window catches the last rays of the sun.

AFSLUITDIJK

You cannot lose your way on the Afsluitdijk. 35 kilometers there or back.

MAASVLAKTE/SOUTH HOLLAND

New land offshore. New roads, new firms, new beaches, new power stations, a new harbour, a new. . .

HET BILDT / FRIESLAND

The Frisians call it the "Bouwhoek". Quiet roads through oversized potato fields. Not a cow in sight.

EUROPOORT / SOUTH HOLLAND

Just like birds, gas and flames find their way into the air.

ALMERE / FLEVOLAND

Towns, villages, farms, factories, roads, canals, drains and pumping engines. The country is being laid out.

ZURICH / FRIESLAND

At different levels one road crosses another. The road above leads to distant places. Beneath you're in the nearest village in no time.

ZURICH / FRIESLAND

The Afsluitdijk on the way to Friesland. Zurich is the first village. Nobody knows what goes on there since the A31 races past it.

PERNIS / SOUTH HOLLAND

The country's second petroleum harbour, on the south bank of the new Maas. Refinery in a foreboding light. A place to work, not to live.

BARTLEHIEM / FRIESLAND

Eleven towns at the waters edge. On skates you can visit them all. Preferably during a race. See who gets there first.

EUROPOORT / SOUTH HOLLAND

Concern, safety and order in this the largest harbour in the world.

MAASVLAKTE / SOUTH HOLLAND

Twenty square kilometers of manmade land. Occupied by a miriad of little firms, five oil refineries and petrochemical industries.

SCHILLAARD / FRIESLAND

A few houses, a single farm and a church tower. Not enough for the train to stop.

VEER OLST / OVERIJSSEL

Twice a year the IJssel overruns its banks. Roads and waterways merge silently and invisibly.

OUD BEYERLAND / SOUTH HOLLAND

The Haringvliet, behind the dike, is no longer tidal. The water is at peace, like the land within the dike.

SCHILLAARD / FRIESLAND

Only in the winter one can see, from afar, that the church is not a church any more. Only the tower of this 16th century building has lived to see our century.

144

MDCCCCLXXXVIII

ISBN 90 6255 362 1

Colophon

Photos: Martin Kers
Lithos: Schipper Fotolitho, Steffenshein-West 30,
1251 WB Laren
Design: Wijnand Camu
Printing: Tesink, Zutphen - The Netherlands